BIG 4

ACCOUNTING - AUDIT

Big 4 Accounting Audit –Interview Tricks & Tips

Featuring a preview into 'Essential Knowledge for a First Year
Audit Staff/Intern at a Big 4 Accounting Firm'

KEVIN HSU

www.stockkevin.com

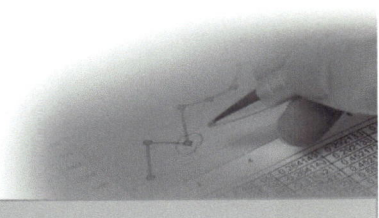

ISBN: 1481098691
ISBN-13: 978-1481098694

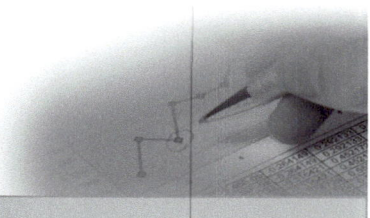

.

Table of Contents

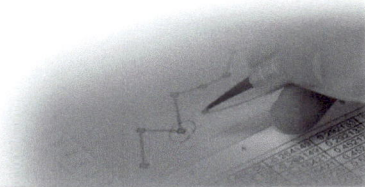

About the Author

Kevin Hsu graduated Cum Laude from University of California, Irvine with a Bachelors of Arts in Economics and Minor in Accounting. He is a Certified Public Accountant and has worked in a Big 4 public accounting firm (i.e. Ernst & Young, KPMG, Deloitte, or PwC) for about three years primarily servicing clients in the credit services and life sciences/pharmaceuticals industries. However, he has experience in the automotive, electronics, and private equity industries as well.

Prior to working in the Big 4, Kevin held a finance position at The Boeing Company. He also spent some time working at an investment banking firm, which focused on mergers and acquisitions. In addition, he is the owner of StockKevin.com, a personal growth, stock trading, and financial savvy site. When he is not working, Kevin enjoys golfing, rock climbing, meditation, and yoga.

What Exactly is Public Accounting?

Most people I meet have no idea what I do for a living. To their credit, most of the time I have no idea what they do for a living either. But, let us help clear the muddy water at least on our end. A typical conversation with a person I just met might go as follows:

Person I just met (Jack/Jill): "Where exactly do you work?"

My reply: "I work at a Big 4 accounting firm."

In the most dull and lethargic tone possibly imaginable coupled with the rolling of the eyes he/she says, "Oh so, you are an accountant, well that's boring.

The boring he/she is thinking of is a different kind of boring I am thinking of. We don't do much accounting in terms of bookkeeping nor do we sit in front of a desk with a calculator crunching numbers. In this day in age, we have Excel for that.

Jack/Jill: "What do you do exactly?"

To which, I calmly reply, "I provide assurance/audit services."

Suddenly there is a moment of excitement. I see Jack/Jill break out in a smile. Perhaps he/she understands what I do after all.

The next words out of his/her mouth are, "Oh, will you do my taxes?" No, I will not do your taxes!

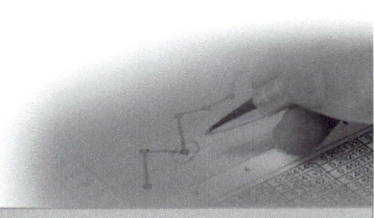

Jack/Jill: "Can you get me out of paying taxes?"

My reply: "No, I cannot."

Jack/Jill: "So, where is your office located?"

My reply: "Typically, I work at the client's site."

Jack/Jill: "Oh, so you are a temp?"

My reply: "No, we just do work at the client site because that is where the information and resources are. We need to test controls and perform certain tests to ensure their financial statements are fairly stated"

How do you explain to someone you just met, what you do? This is a very common question.

The easiest way I can explain it to someone not familiar with the industry is that I review the financial statements of companies. To break it down further, there are companies selling stock in the NYSE, correct? To which you reply yes. When someone buys their stock they are investing in the company; effectively owning a piece of the company.

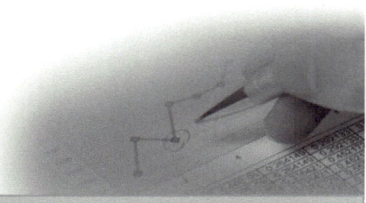

How does the investor know if a company is worth investing in? While there is technical analysis (i.e Fibonacci retracements, moving day averages), usually investors will look at the company's financial statements. Basically how much the company is making, what they own, and where their cash is being used. It is the responsibility of the companies to prepare these financial statements, but how does the investor know that they are being prepared accurately?

They obviously have a huge incentive to overstate their earnings. That is where we come in. We are auditors and we make sure through a series of tests, scoping, and audit methodologies. We determine what is the more effective way and sometimes efficient way to determine that the financials are reasonably stated. What we did here is basically take something most people understand (companies issue stocks) and led them through the thought process of what value the profession adds. Typically, this does the trick.

What are the Benefits of Working in Public Accounting?

You may have heard the horror stories of working late in cramped audit conference rooms, but what are the positives of working in public accounting? In no particular order, here are eight benefits to working in Big 4 public accounting.

1)   Working with high-level individuals

We communicate on a daily to weekly basis with managers, senior managers, controllers, VPs, and sometimes even CFOs. Ultimately the accounting schedules that we perform procedures over are

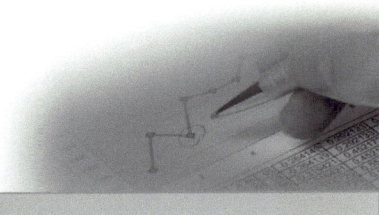

prepared by senior accountants and then reviewed by management. If we need to get an understanding of what the schedule means or what certain figures are derived from, we ask them directly. If you were working in private accounting, you would typically only report to one or a couple individuals. For example, if you were working on the client side, you may only be reporting to the inventory manager or only the revenue manager. If you are in charge of testing the revenue and inventory audit areas, you would have direct communications with the revenue and inventory managers from the client side. As a result you would be exposed to more areas of the balance sheet and income statement, therefore have a higher learning curve. Not only that, but you learn what their job is like and if you would ever follow their paths.

2)   Being in a different locations

 When most people think of an accountant, they see a number crunching person in front of a computer. The moment I told my doctor what I did for a living, he said "lots of numbers huh". While it may be true that we look at numbers, we aren't in the same place day in and day out. As an auditor, we are where the client is. The reason is because we need the client to provide us with answers and supporting documents. If you worked in private accounting, you would be working in the same office and most likely the same cubical all year long. One of the benefits of being in audit is that although you may be on a rough client (i.e long hours or people you don't get along with), you know that it will only be for a couple months or even a couple days. There is light at the end of the tunnel. Similarly, if a job is great, you'll know that all great things eventually come to an end.

3)   Working with young people

When you are spending eleven plus hours of your day with people, you better get along with them. It helps when they are your age and can relate. We often discuss

the latest music and latest trends. It's a mentorship business model, so the senior would coach the experienced associate and the experienced associate the new associate. As we are all more or less computer savvy, it helps that we are on the same level. It truly matters who you are working with.

4)   Working with different people

Big 4 public accounting is an international business. Those who work for the firms  are typically hired directly from university campuses and then are internally trained. As a result, you get a mix of personalities and different ethnic backgrounds. The fact that each team's dynamic differs exposes you to different people. One job you may be working with Jack and Jill who are both type A personalities. While on another job you may we

working with Bill, who is more laid back. Like I mentioned above, if you don't get along with them, you'll know it is only for a couple weeks. If you do, then it's all gravy. Either way, you are put in a position to adapt to people's personalities. This can prove to be useful in the business world.

5)   Managing teams

Seniors typically manage teams comprised of about two to five persons. There are  certain jobs where there will be multiple seniors managing upwards towards ten plus associates. The opportunity to manage individuals after only two years out of college is a tremendous learning opportunity. Not only do you build on leadership skills, but you learn how to adapt to motivate your audit associates. It is rare that companies will allow people who have worked only two years to start managing people.

6)   Reimbursement of mileage and business meals

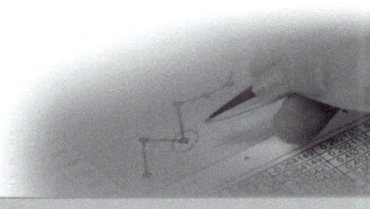

If you do travel, your mileage will be reimbursed at 55.5 cents per mile. That can end up being an extra two hundred to three hundred dollars each paycheck. Of course business meals are expensed and charged to the client. This means you will be able to save a lot of money especially during Busy Season. Typically the team will order dinner during Busy Season because it is expected that you work at least eleven hour days. We usually have a budget of about $25 for dinner, which is enough for a good dinner.

7)   Recession proof so to speak

During the latest recession, a couple of Big 4 firms did lay off employees. However, those individuals who were laid off generally were able to find jobs in private accounting. The reason is because the skills those individuals developed while

working in a Big 4 is highly desirable in the industry. For example, as mentioned previously, most people are given the opportunity to manage staff members as a senior. This means you would be able to develop managerial skills far before your peers have the opportunity to do so. Furthermore, we are trained to meet tight deadlines and have a strong work ethic. This among other desirable skills is what people employers look for. In addition, if we think about it, even if a company is filing for bankruptcy, the accountants are the last to be let go. When does a company know they are going under? They need an accountant to show that in the financial statements. In the end, working in public accounting and more specifically Big 4, opens job opportunities even in the midst of recessions.

8)   Flexibility

When you start to move up the firm, you have more responsibilities including determining the staffing of associates. While interim procedures, which includes controls testing and preliminary substantive work, require

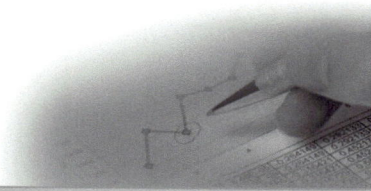

the client's assistance, planning procedures can be done offsite. During this time, which is typically during the summer, depending on your manager you will be allowed to work offsite either at the office or even at home. Managers aren't always on site for all of the day and thus have greater flexibility. This doesn't mean that we don't get our work done; it just means we have a greater window throughout the day to get it done barring any hard deadlines. There aren't that many jobs that will give you that flexibility right out of the gates.

How do I Break into the Industry?
(Including Industry Specific Interview Tips)

The most common way people enter the Big 4 is through on-campus college/university recruiting.

Before you even think about applying for a position at a firm, you should be building your professional network. The best way to do this is to find accounting and finance related clubs on your college campuses More often than not, accounting and finance associations/clubs will host guest speakers from public accounting firms and invite them to speak at club meetings. Typically this provide an opportunity for those who are interested in finding more about public accounting to learn more. On the flipside, firms get a head start on recruiting.

In addition, a great way to learn more about the firm is to attend their firm office tours. These give you a peek into the work environment and give you the opportunity to meet professionals in the industry. But, please understand that more often than not we are not in the office.

The more events you attend and network with a recruiter the more he or she will recognize your face and name. When it comes to submitting your resume for an internship or full-time job, you will be the first person the recruiter thinks of. Typically if you've developed a good enough rapport with him or her, you are almost always guaranteed a first round interview. I've known students who have had subpar GPAs. But because they had a good working relationship with the recruiter, their resumes were pushed through to the first round of interviews.

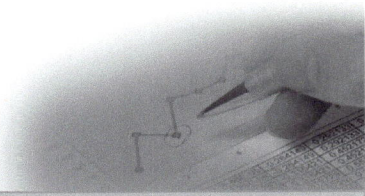

If possible, I would recommend trying to get a position in one of the accounting club/organizations on campus.

More specifically, for obvious reasons, if you found a role that would involve you working directly with the recruiters, that would be ideal. Many of my friends have bypassed first round interviews because they've developed good rapport with a partner and the recruiter through their role as the liaison between the club and the firm. Though this does not happen often, it does happen.

Big 4 firms and even some mid-tiers typically start interviewing the year before they want you to start working. For full-time positions, this typically occurs in the Fall (October/November) of your senior year. Internship positions which are usually are for third years and interviews begin in the Winter (January or February).

Regardless of whether you apply for an internship or a full-time position, the interview formats are similar. Generally speaking, there are at least two rounds of interviews. First you would submit your resume to the firm either via the firm website, through a recruiter, or your on-campus career center. Based on their review of your GPA (grades), coursework, and any internship, they will then invite you to a first round interview. More often than not, this is held on campus, though in many cases this could be over the phone.

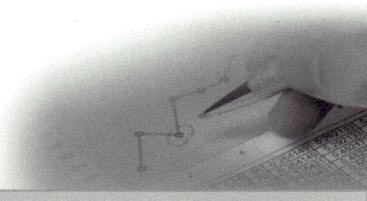

For an on-campus interview, there is usually either a partner or a manager that will come to the career center and hold a thirty minute to an hour interview. The first round interview is largely behavioral question based with very few technical questions if any. They may provide you with a scenario and ask you how you would react or what actions you would take. In addition, they may ask you to describe a time when you've lead a team. You can draw from your group project experiences or if you were involved in a leadership position in either a fraternity or sorority.

A good response would include describing the situation, your role or contribution, and the results of your actions. For example, in my marketing class, the team was assigned a project to create and market a new product. As the team leader, I organized the meeting times and created an agenda based on feedback from the team members. The first agenda included discussion of team members' roles and responsibilities, brainstorming products, what industry we wanted to enter, and other administrative items. As a result the meetings were efficient and effective. We would spend no more than an hour at each meeting. Usually this also included providing updates. If any problems arose we would discuss it as a team to solve the issues. Because of the organization and framework that was provided the team was able to successfully present to the class and professor our marketing plan for the next energy drink.

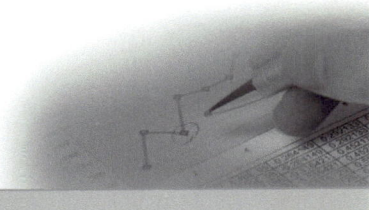

At any point of time, the interviewer may ask follow up questions or probe so to speak. For example, they may ask what issues came up during these meetings? How did you and your team go about solving the issue? One of the best ways to approach answering these questions is to first tell the interview that you would understand the issue. The reason this is effective is because as an auditor we are always put in difficult and unusual scenarios. This is especially the case as we move from client to client. What the interviewer is looking for that you are able to think quick on your feet and have the ability to understand the situation and propose a solution or know where to find the solution.

The second thing the interviewer is looking for is if you are able to talk to the client. The best way for them to gauge this is through your conversation with the interviewer. This is another point; personally I believe the interview should not be a question and answering session. What I mean by this is that if all you are doing is strictly responding to the interviewer's questions you are doing something wrong. The interview should be like a dialogue, there should be some small talk. If you can get the interviewer to talk about his or her interests, then that is when you've hit the money. Even better is if you can relate to his or her interests and provide some examples of what you've done.

People like people that are similar to them or at least can relate. If you are a college student and being interviewed by a manager or partner, chances are there will be an age gap or generation gap. Some of the topics you can bring up are travelling and food. Manager and partners travel a great more deal than associates and senior associates.

Most of them have traveled abroad to countries such as Argentina, parts of Europe and even Asia. If you've traveled abroad, you can bring those experiences in to the conversation/interview.

There will be time towards the end of the interview where the interviewer will ask if you have any questions. It is always a best practice to say that you do and what better time than to ask them

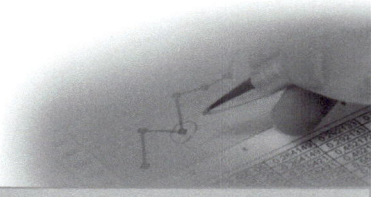

about their travels. This way it shows that you are not only interested in the position, but the interviewer as well. At the end of the interview, I would thank them for their time and ask for their business card. That way you will be able to follow up and send a thank you note. Usually an email is sufficient. I would wait till the end of the day or early next morning to send the email. Most people will send the email right after the interview, but if the person receives ten different emails all at once, it is less likely that your email will be seen. Also, they tend to make their decisions rather quickly. Usually the email thank you note will not make or break your chances of an offer. The thank you email is more of a common courtesy and reinforcement of a good interview.

Occasionally your interview may be over the phone This happens if you did not go through on campus interviews and are an experienced hire. Depending on the firm, they have a screening call which is probably ten to fifteen minutes. Then they'll schedule an actual phone interview. If that is successful, they will bring you in for an office interview with at least two managers/senior managers and a partner. This may vary depending on if there are enough managers and partners available that day. What happens is that the recruiter sets the dates for when the interviews are held and then reach out to the firm itself to ask if there are people who can fill the interview roles at the specified dates.

This is different from if you were to work for a firm and you have one immediate manager, typically if you applied for that position you would interview with your immediate manager and your boss' boss. In the Big 4 you have many managers, so at the end of the day it doesn't matter who interviews you because you'll likely be working with a number of different people.

After first round  interviews, you'll probably find out from the recruiter about a week later whether or not you've made it to second rounds. If you don't hear about before then I would reach out to show that you are still interested. In most cases, the interviewer will tell you when you should expect to hear back.

Second round interviews are held at the firms. It is usually half the day; meaning you'll likely get in at 9:00AM and leave after lunch. The recruiter will give you background on the firm and a chance to get to know the other interviewees. People are usually anxious and nervous the first time they step into the firm. Especially since the environment is different from that of which you are used to. For example, if you are a college student. The first few hours might be ice breakers and the firm really just selling them to you. They may have partners come in and talk about the firm and their experiences. After a couple hours they will pair you up with an audit assistant or senior auditor who will take you to your two to three interviews.

You'd be surprised by the size of the manager and partner's offices. They are not as big as you'd imagine and again it is because most of the time they are not in their offices but at client sites.

These interviews are to see if you are a fit for the firm's culture. In other words, if you can get along with the firm's employees or if you can hold a conversation with the client, then you will fit their bill.

Still, they may ask you behavioral questions depending on the manager who interviews you. There are very detailed managers and managers that are more or less high level thinkers. Some interviewers will ask you technical questions, but they don't expect you to know how to audit. The firm will teach all that, but they do except you to know the balance sheet, income statement, auditing, etc. is. Basically I would review what you've learned in class because the interviewers will know what classes you've taken and that is fair game. When in doubt, let them know that you will get back to them. If they ask you a technical question you do not know the answer to, I would write it down and tell them that you will follow up and research the answer before getting back to them. Or if you have an idea of what the answer might be, I would say it but then say that you will research the issue more and get the answer.

Then after the interview day, I would go and research the issue and follow up via email. After your first interview, your interview buddy they've assigned with take you to your second

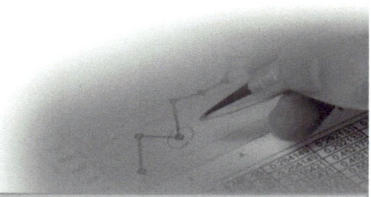

interview. The format is the same as the first interview and usually is about forty five minutes to an hour long. Afterwards your buddy will take you out to lunch with a group of other interviewees and their buddies. Although this is not as crucial as the interview itself, your buddy is also looking to see if you can interact with them and would fit in if you were on their team. It is a time for you to get to know them, but also understand that they have input into whether or not you get hired as well. It is probably a good idea to brush up on dinner/lunch etiquette.

After lunch, you'll head back to the firm and the recruiter will give you some closing remarks and let you know when you should find out. Sometimes the firm will make the decision the day off or they might wait till the following week. It is going to vary. If they do not tell you already, it is a good question to ask the recruiter or interviewer. When they let you know whether or not you received an offer they usually have the recruiter or the partner reach out to you directly. Don't feel pressured to accept the first offer you get. It is okay to let them know that you are still waiting on other offers or you need time to think about it but ask them when they need to know your decision by.

There will likely be  paperwork to fill out when you accept your offer, but your recruiter should be able to guide you through what needs to be completed and by which date. Just make sure you mark the important dates on your calendar.

However if you are not in college or attending school, an alternative way is to come in as an experienced hire. Use your connections to work at a mid or local tier firm (e.g. McGladrey, BDO, White Nelson) and then try to get an interview at a Big 4. The interview format may differ slightly from the above, but generally speaking the principles documented above still apply.

SNEAK PREVIEW

Essential Knowledge for a First Year Audit Staff/Intern at a Big 4 Accounting Firm

TRUE INSIDER'S PERSPECTIVE ON BIG 4 ACCOUNTING

CONTENTS

About The Author

Kevin Hsu graduated Cum Laude from University of California, Irvine with a Bachelors of Arts in Economics and Minor in Accounting. He is a Certified Public Accountant and has worked in a Big 4 public accounting firm (i.e. Ernst & Young, KPMG, Deloitte, or PwC) for about three years primarily servicing clients in the credit services and life sciences/pharmaceuticals industries. However, he has experience in the automotive, electronics, and private equity industries as well.

Prior to working in the Big 4, Kevin held a finance position at The Boeing Company. He also spent some time working at an investment banking firm, which focused on mergers and acquisitions. In addition, he is the owner of StockKevin.com, a personal growth, stock trading, and financial savvy site. When he is not working, Kevin enjoys golfing, rock climbing, meditation, and yoga.

HAT TYPES OF CAREERS ARE IN ACCOUNTING?

When you think of an accountant, typically, you think of someone who prepares tax returns or is a pure number cruncher. While this might have been true in the past, nowadays we have Microsoft Excel to help us crunch numbers. But, accounting is much more than that. Stricter government regulations such as the implementation of the Sarbanes-Oxley Act have paved the way for greater demands in different careers within the accounting field. Below are a few sub-categories within the accounting field to consider.

Audit: Auditors perform procedures to ensure company's financial statements are free from material misstatements. In addition, they ensure that the financial statements accurately reflect the financial performance of the company they are auditing. Banks and lenders request companies be audited because they want to be reassured that companies they lend to will be able to pay their debts. Public companies file reports such as the 10K and 10Q with the SEC. Investors factor into their decision making process the information in these reports. Naturally, companies will have an incentive to overstate their assets and understate their liabilities. Therefore it is important to have a third party, such as an auditor to ensure that the banks and investors are protected.

Tax: Tax professionals prepare tax returns both on an individual and corporate basis. This includes international, federal, state, and local tax returns. In these economic times, companies are looking to reduce their tax liabilities and make  better investment decisions. Tax regulations are constantly changing. This is largely due to the direction the government decides to take the economy. For example, the housing market been on a decline in recent years. In order to mitigate this situation, the government has decided to provide tax credits to first time homeowners to boost the housing market. Tax professionals are aware of such recent developments and would be able to effectively advise individuals.

Information Technology (IT): As the world moves towards more and more sophisticated software systems, the need for individuals with IT knowledge continues to grow alongside it. Accounting systems' design complexities have increased in recent years and require extensive knowledge to troubleshoot. Professionals continue to design and implement advanced software systems. Individuals with skills to manipulate, design, and implement such systems are extremely valuable to companies.

Internal Audit: Although similar in duties to an external auditor, internal auditors focus on ensuring their company's internal controls are functioning properly. In some cases, they will perform similar procedures to that of an external auditor. An internal auditor is directly associated with their company and thus not considered a third party. Therefore, companies will have to employ another company to ensure their financial statements are free from material misstatements. Where internal auditor's value lies is in the fact that they will be able to large issues before they reach the external auditors. Therefore, cut down the work needed from external auditors, effectively reducing audit fees.

Forensics: Accounting professionals perform procedures to detect white collar crime such as fraud, tax evasion, and embezzlement.

International Focus: With exception to countries like the United States, much of the world is under IFRS (International Financial Reporting Standards). Globalization has moved the United States to consider IFRS Standards. There have been advanced talks regarding the inclusion of IFRS standards in the CPA exam. Professionals with IFRS experience will become valuable to companies within the United States as well as across the globe in the coming years.

Consulting: This involves financial planning, organizational restructuring, and management tactics. Individuals will leverage prior years' data and knowledge of the current business environment to plan for the future.

General Accounting: Accountants are responsible for general ledgers, trial balances, financial statements and other general accounting issues. Often these same individuals will be responsible for closing the books at year end. Furthermore, it is not uncommon to see reconciliations from the detail listings to the trial balances be a part of their duties.

The first couple days you are fine, but after a couple weeks of this you start to feel the effects. Suddenly your one cup of coffee per day is not enough and three cups are needed to stay awake. It's an intense experience for someone who has not been through it before. You are with the same people for eleven plus hours. We are not talking about each of you having your own personal space. We are all sharing each other's space. You can see that if you don't get along with someone, it could make your experience a long one. Time passes very quickly as it is, but when you are as busy as you are during busy season; it seems to go by twice as fast. For example, you come into work, get set up, answer emails, coordinate meetings, perform some detailed tests, then all of a sudden its lunch. After lunch you detail test, coach associates, answer emails, perform more detailed tests. Then suddenly it's five, but because it busy season you probably won't even notice. Five o' clock becomes six then seven and then nine and then twelve. The day is over, but you could still be in front of your computer. Finally when you retire for the night, just know you will have to do it again the next day.

If you think that you can catch up on the weekends, think again. This is not always the case, but more likely than not you will probably be working on the weekends. These are typically not full days, but can be depencing on your jobs. You can see why it is important to push work forward and do as much as you can when it is not busy. I can't say that busy season is something you can prepare for mentally. Unless you've gone through the experience, something similar, or much worse; you can only anticipate how you will react. Truthfully, it is not about the hours. It is more about the amount of work, pressure, and the fact that you are with the same people for countless hours. It makes a big difference if you are in a room with someone you are coworker friendly with versus someone that you don't get along with.

The following is a description of a busy season day as experienced by an Assurance Associate at one of the Big Four firms:

7:00am - I roll out of my bed and hit the alarm simultaneously. I head to the kitchen and mix some instant oatmeal mix with hot water and grab a piece of bread. As I wait for my oatmeal to cool, I dress for work and make sure I have my laptop, wallet, keys, phone, and sack lunch. Seven minutes in, my oatmeal has not cooled yet, but in the interest of time, I decide to finish it anyways. Afterwards, I brush my teeth, do my hair, and shave.

7:30am - I realize that I am already late, so I rush out of the house only to unsurprisingly hit freeway traffic.

Individuals on a team have assigned 'steps' or standard procedures you perform, however it's not as simple as ABC. If you have no experience with auditing you will not be able to follow these procedures. The reason is that these procedures are written out for individuals who have audit experience! As a first year you gain exposure to cash, property, plant, and equipment, accounts payable, and various less risky areas. You start to gain a grasp of accounting in practice and you begin to realize that it's not as straightforward as it was written in your college textbooks. You'll start to see that the excel files your client work with are unorganized and difficult to decipher. For someone who is not already familiar with the excel file, they can be extremely difficult to follow. They have numbers all over the place and numbers that are hardcoded. There is no manual or guide as to what is going on with the spreadsheet. The only way to gain an understanding over it is to have the client explain to you or have a senior associate coach you.

Effectively you are checking the work of some let us say forty year old manager who has tons more experience than you do and actually has a clue of what is going on. How do you think they feel when you come in and challenge their work?

I can't imagine anyone who welcomes auditors. You'll get push back from the client more times than not, but they understand the audit doesn't get done if they don't cooperate with you. Still, for whatever reason, they will make it as difficult for you as possible. My biggest advice I can give is to research the topic to get background on the issue before you speak to the client. This can be looking at prior year databases, firm research resources, and asking your senior.

You will be able to order Essential Knowledge for a First Year Audit Staff/Intern at a Big 4 Accounting firm on Amazon.

Alternatively you can visit www.stockkevin.com and purchase the copy at a discounted price.

www.ingramcontent.com/pod-product-compliance
Lightning Source LLC
Chambersburg PA
CBHW041212180526
45172CB00006B/1242